# Who Do I Tell?

Tracey L. Tindall

MW01538713

Copyright © 2016 Tracey L. Tindall.

All rights reserved. No part of this book may be used or reproduced by any means, graphic, electronic, or mechanical, including photocopying, recording, taping or by any information storage retrieval system without the written permission of the author except in the case of brief quotations embodied in critical articles and reviews.

WestBow Press books may be ordered through booksellers or by contacting:

WestBow Press
A Division of Thomas Nelson & Zondervan
1663 Liberty Drive
Bloomington, IN 47403
www.westbowpress.com
1 (866) 928-1240

Because of the dynamic nature of the Internet, any web addresses or links contained in this book may have changed since publication and may no longer be valid. The views expressed in this work are solely those of the author and do not necessarily reflect the views of the publisher, and the publisher hereby disclaims any responsibility for them.

Author photo by Rachel Parker Photography
Illustrations by Stephen Baker

ISBN: 978-1-5127-5055-3 (sc)
ISBN: 978-1-5127-5056-0 (e)

Print information available on the last page.

WestBow Press rev. date: 08/19/2016

WESTBOW
PRESS®
A DIVISION OF THOMAS NELSON
& ZONDERVAN

# ACKNOWLEDGEMENT

To the little girl I once was – be the change!

To those who have hurt me, I forgive you because my God forgives me. -Matthew 6:14

For all who have given me guidance and opportunities along this journey – Thank you with all of my heart! I have some amazing teachers, friends, and mentors in my life!

A special thank you to Amber Gallagher for your friendship and encouragement in my writing endeavors! And to Carolyn Slotten, an all-time favorite professor at Miami University in Oxford, Ohio, who supported and encouraged my writing.

Thank you to The Lord, our God and Savior, for allowing me to serve others and give back in this way.

Lastly, and certainly not least – to my husband, Jason and our three children, Adrielle, Jason Jr., and Zach – I love you all so very much! Thank you for making so many sacrifices for me to get where I am today. Your support means the world to me.

Penny is a little girl that loves school and her friends; they play outside after school almost every day. Sometimes, they jump rope or draw with sidewalk chalk. Her best friend is Anna, and if it's rainy, they go inside Anna's house to play.

At school, Penny's favorite subjects are English and Gym. She likes to read and write poems in English class. Once, she wrote a sweet poem for Anna.

In gym class, Anna and Penny play games with their other friends. They have a lot of fun. On the last day of school, they have Field Day. They are excited for that day.

Penny lives with her mom and step-father. She also has a younger brother and a furry white dog. She loves her family and her dog very much.

There is a swing-set in Penny's back yard with a big yellow slide. Penny's brother loves for her to push him in the swing until his toes go high into the sky.

Penny's step-father has been married to her mom for two years. He is a nice man. He plays with her brother, and sometimes takes him to games on the weekends.

Every week, Penny gets a new bucket of sidewalk chalk from her step-dad.

Sometimes, when Penny's mom isn't home, her step-dad likes to play the Tickle Game. He chases Penny and her brother around the house. He tickles them until they laugh really loud.

Penny's brother gets bored very easily and sometimes goes to his room when their step-father is chasing Penny for the Tickle Game.

Penny thinks the Tickle Game is fun at first. After awhile, her step-father starts to touch her in places on her body that are private. Private parts on your body are what your swimsuit covers.

Sometimes, Penny's step-father comes into her bedroom and touches her private parts. He tells her to be very quiet so that her mom and brother won't hear. Penny is scared, but she doesn't know who to tell.

At school, Penny keeps thinking about her step-father and how he touches her sometimes. She has a hard time paying attention in school. She wants to tell her teacher or Anna, but she is afraid she will be in trouble. Her step-father says it's a secret and she should never tell anyone.

Penny doesn't have fun with her friends anymore. Anna asks her every day why she isn't laughing and playing, and she wants to tell Anna, but her step-father would be angry.

Penny's step-father won't let her go outside and have fun anymore. Her mom has been working late, so her step-father takes care of Penny and her brother most of the time.

Penny wants to tell someone about her step-father, but who does she tell?

Anna talked to her mom today. She is worried about Penny because she doesn't laugh and play in gym class anymore, she doesn't go outside and make chalk pictures, and Penny barely speaks to Anna anymore.

Anna told Penny that she talked to her mom because she's worried about her. Then, Penny told her she has a secret, but she's afraid to tell anyone. Penny wants to tell someone what her step-father is doing, but who can she tell?

Today at school, Penny's favorite teacher met with her. The teacher let Penny know that he can tell something must be bothering her and he wants to help. Penny is still afraid of getting in trouble, because she knows her step-father will be very angry if she tells the secret.

Penny didn't tell the secret to her teacher today. She went home after school where her step-father was waiting.

Penny's step-father asked her if she had told their secret. She was very afraid and shook her head "no". Her step-father touched her private areas again today. Penny is so afraid and wants to tell, but who does she tell? Penny doesn't want her mom to be mad at her when she tells someone that her step-father is touching her private parts. Penny's mom loves her step-father very much.

Penny is sad and feels alone. Who does she tell?

Penny got to visit Anna after school today. Penny's mom is home from work early and let her go to Anna's house to play.

As the two best friends took a snack break, Anna's mom talked to the girls about school and the upcoming Field Day. Anna told Penny she misses playing with her every day after school. Anna's mom could see that Penny was upset and seemed afraid. Penny wants to tell someone about her secret, but who can she tell?

Penny was very scared, and she started to cry. She told Anna's mom about her secret; that her step-father touches the private parts on her body. Anna's mom told Penny that no matter who touches her in the private places on her body, it is NEVER her fault. Penny is glad that she could finally tell the secret.

Every week, Penny talks to a counselor. Penny has no more secrets. She knows she isn't alone and how her step-father touched her was wrong.

Penny doesn't have to keep secrets about someone touching her private body parts any longer. She can tell her mom, a teacher or another trusted adult. If someone touches her the way her step-father did, she knows IT IS OK TO TELL.

Thank you for reading Penny's story. Penny wants you to know that if someone is touching you like her step-father did or in another way that makes you feel uncomfortable, you can tell.

IT IS OK TO TELL.

**You can also get help by calling one of these numbers below:**

National Child Abuse Hotline
1-800-4-A-Child
1-800-422-4453
www.childhelp.org/hotline/resources-kids/


The National Center for Missing and Exploited Children
1-800-THE-LOST
1-800-843-5678
www.missingkids.com

CPSIA information can be obtained
at www.ICGtesting.com
Printed in the USA
LVOW05s1920020916

503023LV00013B/16/P

9 781512 750553